Unless otherwise stated all scriptures and quotations are taken from the King James Version.

Alphamight LLC

kazeemo@100bconline.com

Table of Contents

Preface

This compilation of wisdom cookies is to be taken and used as bible study material on wisdom for daily living. My aim is to use these as eye opener for you and believing that the Holy Spirit would enable you to personally look and dig deeper into these insights for a better and glorious experience with life and God.

No nation is stronger than its spiritual forces. Only the church is stronger than those spiritual forces. By Kathryn Khurmah

Bring this to family level. No family is stronger than the spiritual forces ruling their family realm. This is what Jesus was talking about when he said you must bind the strong man (spiritual forces) before you can be able to set its captives free. Only empowered Christians by God are stronger than the spiritual forces ruling his/her family spiritual realm.

Take note of the book of Is 6:9

Not in seeing but what you perceived (Jn 4:19).

Not in hearing but what you understand.

Not in what you are saying but what you think (thoughts).

That is, what you see is not as important as to what and how you perceived it.

And what you hear is not as important as to what and how you understand it (this is why Jesus spoke in parables, get wisdom, get understand).

And what comes out of your mouth is not as important as to what and how you think. God answers us based on what we perceive, think and understand.

God answers the blind by what they perceive. While they were still thinking I will answer their prayers (this is how God answers the dumb). God answers the deaf by what they understand.

Cookies for Breaking Forth: The Tribe of Celebrity

In Genesis 2 and 3, when God created Adam and Eve, they were highly celebrated and attracted the attention of all creation and even God visited and followed them in their social space which was the garden of Eden.

And then suddenly the serpent showed up to bring them down. Till today, the celebrated personality still suffers attacks from serpents. When a man's life attracts the goodness of God in the place where God placed him, be it vocation, career, or marriage, that man will be celebrated by friends, colleagues, or nations and for that, the serpent is ever very close. As soon as God announced Jesus at river Jordan, the Devil followed him. When the Devil saw how God celebrated Job and Job's influence and contributions to his generation, the Devil wasted no time for an opportunity to strike Job. Celebrities need our prayers.

Celebrities are fast becoming a class or tribe of their own. Unfortunately, this tribe has its challenges and faces great opposition from powerful, political, and religious people.

From ancient times, we have seen political and religious group leaders hate to see an individual excelling in fame and also pulling crowds and followers. When ordinary people celebrate and follow you, it is a threat to them, and feared you would soon be more powerful than the nation.

As an individual when you start influencing to change or alter government policies or laws, ordinary people begin to celebrate you and then you find yourself in danger with the powerful both political and religious.

1 Samuel 18: 5 -7

And David went out whithersoever Saul sent him, and behaved himself wisely: and Saul set him over the men of war, and he was accepted in the sight of all the people, and also in the sight of Saul's servants. And it came to pass as they came when David was returned from the slaughter of the Philistine, that the women came out of all cities of Israel, singing and dancing, to meet King Saul, with tabrets, with joy, and with instruments of musick. And the women answered one another as they played, and said, Saul, hath slain his thousands, and David his ten thousand.

David returned from war with success and victory and his fame spread and was celebrated and accepted by the people. His victory pulled crowds and followership. He suddenly became a celebrity within a short time. But the king was offended

1 Samuel 18: 8 - 9

And Saul was very wroth, and the saying displeased him; and he said, They have ascribed unto David ten thousand, and to me, they have ascribed but thousands: and what can he have more but the kingdom? And Saul eyed David from that day and forward.

There is always a fear among political and religious leaders when a single individual pulls crowds or is powerful and influential among the people. Especially, when that individual has no known political or religious base. Jesus also experienced this with the Pharisees and Sadducees. Jesus became a celebrity and very common among ordinary and lowly people because of his outstanding miracles and healing ministry and so the religious leaders in those days feared he was having so much influence. And they hated Jesus for this.

John 12: 17 - 19

The people therefore that were with him when he called Lazarus out of his grave and raised him from the dead, bare record. For this cause, the people also met him, and for that, they heard that he had done this miracle. The Pharisees therefore said among themselves, Perceive ye how ye prevail nothing? behold, the world is gone after him

Regarding the apostles, the religious leaders of those days feared greatly the influence of the apostles on ordinary people. Hence, they never gave them rest.

Acts 4: 16 - 17

saying, What shall we do to these men? For that indeed a notable miracle hath been done by them is manifest to all them that dwell in Jerusalem; and we cannot deny it. But that it spread no further among the people, let us straitly threaten them, that they speak henceforth to no man in this name.

Celebrities have always been a source of great fear for political or religious leaders due to their powerful influence on the people. These leaders fear competition and would not want to see an individual having more influence over ordinary people than any political or religious group or party.

John 7: 30 - 32

Then they sought to take him: but no man laid hands on him, because his hour had not yet come. And many of the people believed in him, and said, When Christ cometh, will he do more miracles than these which this man hath done? The Pharisees heard that the people murmured such things concerning him, and the Pharisees and the chief priests sent officers to take him.

Take it or leave it, being a celebrity comes with a price. You might end up being more powerful and influential than some religious or political group. Even some counties, states, or nations might struggle to catch up with your level of influence among the people.

So, also in the church, a young pastor or a deacon or any church member can be so full of grace, loved, and celebrated by the church members so much that the senior pastor can be pushed into envy or hatred thinking you would likely snatch their members away.

So, how do you keep yourself safe in a society like this? Form or operate within a group, do not do anything in isolation or individual settings. It is much easier for political or religious groups to bring down any individual celebrity than to fight a class or group of celebrities.

If Jesus had been part of any religious group, whether the Pharisees or Sadducees, it would have been difficult for any other religious group to fight him successfully. We can look at the following celebrities in our midst today.

Myles Munroe was a powerful celebrity, but his influence was individualistic among the high and low in society, not through a known church body or group. The church was weak in his school of thots, but he was strong. He had the opportunity to dine all over with political leaders and the United Nations. This exposed him to the powerful, in the society.

Oh, see TD Jakes, a celebrity pastor, pulls crowds but he was mostly seen among common men. What wisdom. Staying among those who celebrate him the most ensures his safety. Little wonder the Pharisees could not arrest Jesus in the daytime when he was mostly among the common people who celebrated and loved him. They feared revolts. But still, Jesus never trusted men, he threaded with care. TD Jakes must also not trust his life with men. He needs our prayers too.

What about Jack Ma, he was getting too powerful as an individual and a celebrity businessman. But China had to curtail him. He was threatened and had to readjust and caution the way he talked openly.

Another person is Elon Musk, a celebrity, and powerful individual who can influence government policies already. His father cried out recently, fearing his son might be killed due to Elon's influence beyond ordinary people. He needs our prayers.

If celebrities come together and form a tribe. Speaking as a tribe, not individuals doing their own thing the way they like, then can they live to change or challenge laws without fear of being silenced and then be able to help common men.

Hey, Donald Trump is a celebrity and powerful individual. If Trump had not been part of any political party and talked the way he talks, he would have been silenced for long. He succeeded in using a platform to express himself. His political party doesn't have much influence among ordinary American people, no, not as much to pull crowds and followers without Trump. Pray for him.

The Devil's goal is always to attempt to use celebrities, their lifestyle, their weakness and their insufficiencies to shame the wisdom of God for entrusting them with such grace and blessings. Condemn no man, until you have survived a generation of celebrated season without ever falling into the Devil's tricks.

The main challenges and battles facing celebrity personalities are the spirit of darkness and the spirit of sexual immoralities. They constantly have to contend or war against these forces and the only one who can stand is he whom God helped.

This is why Paul the apostle said, we wrestle not flesh and blood but against principalities and power and spiritual wickedness in high places. Learn to pray rather than condemn.

In the book of Genesis, God created everything quietly, all other beings suddenly saw that God had done something. But for man, God announced ahead before creating man. He said, "Let us make man".

The whole heavens and earth (both the good and evil) attentions were drawn to man. That announcement alone made man a light that cannot be hidden and both good and evil must test man out.

Genesis 1:26

And God said, Let us make man in our image, after our likeness: and let them have dominion over the fish of the sea, and over the fowl of the air, and over the cattle, and over all the earth, and over every creeping thing that creepeth upon the earth.

Also in 1 Peter 1:12, we are told of angels desire

1 Peter 1:12

Unto whom it was revealed, that not unto themselves, but unto us they did minister the things, which are now reported unto you by them that have preached the gospel unto you with the Holy Ghost sent down from heaven; which things the angels desire to look into.

So, each time a celebrity manifests on earth the angels (the righteous and evil) desire to investigate who that is, that is shaking the earth. Hence, celebrities attract fans, their fans can be separated into two groups. The good fans and the evil fans. The evil fans would go through any length to destroy them physically and spiritually. Just like Judas went through several miles to betray Jesus Christ.

While the good fans only rant or talk with their mouths and do nothing to protect and preserve their celebrities. They only support with their mouths and don't see it as their responsibility to fast and pray for their celebrities. Just like Peter and the other apostles who could not stand with Jesus for 1 hour to pray for his life in the garden. This is what our celebrities suffer these days. As a matter of fact, the good fans should have a dedicated day to fast and pray for their celebrities. And when terrible things happen, they are quick to say we don't know what is killing these celebrities these days.

Cookies for Dominion: Knowing When to Invade New Territory

In Genesis 1 God created heaven and the earth. God perceived it was time to break new ground. That is to explore new territory.

Knowing when to migrate to a new territory is a great blessing. It could be moving from one location to another moving from one profession to another moving from one employer to another or delving into new skill areas. Many times, to survive and be successful, you must keep breaking new ground.

Jeremiah 8:7

Yea, the stork in the heaven knoweth her appointed times; and the turtle and the crane and the swallow observe the time of their coming; but my people know not the judgment of the LORD

When birds sense a famine, drought, hunger, or the environment becomes hostile and they sense trouble coming, they migrate to other locations to survive and breed or nest. They leave everything behind to start a life and build where they can survive and later return to their original location if conditions change. When birds feel threatened in a place, they move away and never return. Threat to life and existence is an indication it is time to move to another place to survive.

Not only birds, but all other creatures of nature, plants, and animals alike all keep migrating when there is a need for survival. This is how God gives a signal for them to move. But humans rarely understand this judgment of God.

Humans are afraid of uncertainties; they think moving away means quitting and lack of faith. All other creatures do not fear uncertainties. They just wake up and live their lives and God takes care of them. Little wonder Jesus said that the lilies are clothed by God and birds of the air, neither work nor toil, but God feeds them. Because they never had any fear of uncertainties. Unfortunately, men rather opt to endure pain and failure, hoping for improvement while God had wished they would move. This is the reason many would remain poor or even die still hoping for a change.

 The world is not where you come to LIVE, but a place to SURVIVE. You must keep moving to ensure and maintain your survival. Species (birds, humans, plants) migrate during hostile weather or environments to survive.

Therefore, they must be aggressive in spirit, invasive, and indomitable to survive. The tower of Babel was built to resist or stop migration, but God scattered them. You don't settle down when you are to keep moving.

Gen 11: 1 - 4

And the whole earth was of one language, and of one speech. And it came to pass, as they journeyed from the east, that they found a plain in the land of Shinar; and they dwelt there. And they said one to another, Go to, let us make brick, and burn them throughly. And they had brick for stone, and slime had they for morter. And they said, Go to, let us build us a city and a tower, whose top may reach unto heaven; and let us make us a name, lest we be scattered abroad upon the face of the whole earth.

Abram migrated to survive in Egypt, he did not go there to live. When Abram entered Canaan, he was moving from one location to another location.

Genesis 12: 10 - 11

And there was a famine in the land: and Abram went down into Egypt to sojourn there; for the famine was grievous in the land.

Abraham moved to new territories during the famine. God did not condemn him for looking for greener pastures. He didn't ask him to use faith to overcome difficult times like famine. God led him to Canaan; He knew Abraham was in that city before allowing famine and yet still permitted Abram to run away from famine and from the same promised land. Yet Abraham remains the father of faith. We must wake up as believers.

Isaac also moved to new territories during a famine.

Genesis 26: 1 - 3

And there was a famine in the land, beside the first famine that was in the days of Abraham. And Isaac went unto Abimelech king of the Philistines unto Gerar. And the LORD appeared unto him, and said, Go not down into Egypt; dwell in the land which I shall tell thee of: Sojourn in this land, and I will be with thee, and will bless thee; for unto thee, and unto thy seed, I will give all these countries, and I will perform the oath which I sware unto Abraham thy father

Famine caused Abraham, Isaac, and Jacob to move to Egypt and the land of the Philistines. They moved away from the promised land. Do they lack faith? Nay. Was God not able to supply their needs during famine in Canaan? Nay. Migration has always been an instrument for sustaining lives, and it remains a survival channel.

The Israelites migrated to Egypt to survive and then became invasive. They later returned to Canaan wealthy. Stop being stubborn.

David moved to new territories when the going was tough and when his life was in danger.

1 Samuel 27: 4

And it was told Saul that David was fled to Gath: and he sought no more again for him

1 Samuel 23: 13

So David and his men, about six hundred in all, left Keilah. They went wherever they could go. Then Saul was told, "David has escaped from Keilah!" So he gave up the campaign.

Even our Lord Jesus moved to new territories when rejected in any place.

He also told us to move to another city when we felt unwelcome in any place. That is, when the environment becomes hostile.

Matthew 10:23

But when they persecute you in this city, flee ye into another: for verily I say unto you, Ye shall not have gone over the cities of Israel, till the Son of man be come

The apostles moved to other cities when Jerusalem became hostile to them. The apostles and early Christians were scattered abroad due to threats and insecurities to their lives. This was how the gospel spread.

Acts 8: 3 - 5

As for Saul, he made havock of the church, entering into every house, and haling men and women committed them to prison. Therefore they that were scattered abroad went every where preaching the word. Then Philip went down to the city of Samaria, and preached Christ unto them.

Therefore, God is not against migration. Your blessing is from above, I know, but if He that is above in His wisdom chose to bless you abroad, is that not awesome? Move when God says move, do not act as if you have faith more than your God. Can you imagine now why God asked Joseph to relocate to Egypt with Jesus Christ to save Jesus's life?

Jesus talking about his movement from one place to the other made this statement below.

Matthew 8:20

And Jesus saith unto him, The foxes have holes, and the birds of the air have nests; but the Son of man hath not where to lay his head

And Jesus' length of stay in a place, depends on the comfortability and how he was received in the environment.

Your country or local space is where you LIVE not where you SURVIVE. Foreign land or space is where you SURVIVE and not where you LIVE.

If you struggle to survive in your country, you will remain poor, because it is a place where you must live. But if you survive or migrate to survive in a foreign land, you will become rich. If you go to a foreign land to live without the survival instincts, you will be poor.

Abraham went for survival in Egypt. He was rich and returned to Canaan to live. Note he migrated to Canaan to live and wherever you choose to live is also your resting place (where you can also die). Elimelech went out of Canaan initially to survive but he ended up living by doing nothing and died in a foreign land, his family had to return to Canaan still poor, and could not afford daily food, Ruth had to go to work in Boaz field to survive, Ruth 1: 1 - 10. Do not forget also that Jacob left Canaan to survive in the house of Laban, his uncle when his life was threatened by Esau. He returned with great wealth after several years.

Every single individual that migrated as recorded in the bible had a survival spirit and so they returned rich except Elimelech. There was no evidence that Elimelech had a farm, cattle, or animals, not even a small business to his credit. He did not plant any fruit or corn. The survival spirit was not in him.

Even when God scattered the Israelites abroad, He gave them a survival spirit, to be great and wealthy in a foreign land. Also later returned to their land of Canaan. He told them to build houses, do farming, and do business in Babylon and give their sons and daughters in marriage.

Jeremiah 29: 4 - 7

Thus saith the LORD of hosts, the God of Israel, unto all that are carried away captives, whom I have caused to be carried away from Jerusalem unto Babylon; Build ye houses, and dwell in them; and plant gardens, and eat the fruit of them; Take ye wives, and beget sons and daughters; and take wives for your sons, and give your daughters to husbands, that they may bear sons and daughters; that ye may be increased there, and not diminished. And seek the peace of the city whither I have caused you to be carried away captives and pray unto the LORD for it: for in the peace thereof shall ye have peace.

Yu don't become poor in a land you go to survive but you can be rich or poor where you choose to live. Be invasive and also seek the peace of the land. Being wise and not be destructive is the wisdom key you must apply.

Now, hear this, God can be gracious to some, where the foreign land they went to survive also became the land where they live. And they will enjoy both wealth and peace in that same land.

To discover great wealth, the four lepers had to migrate, running away from famine. If they stay, they die if they move, there is a likelihood of survival. So, they took the risk. Behold great wealth awaited them outside the gate entrance (that is, at the border), 2 Kings 7: 1 - 10.

The choice of survival pushed them to move out. Your natural habitat or your country is a place where you are meant to live, not a place where you are meant to survive.

The wisdom: Build and Plant where you are.

Invest where you are and when it is time to return home, sell or dispose of it and take all with you back home if need be. Do not send hard-earned money or resources home for anyone to build for you, for a house you may likely not see, or live in, or for a house your children will likely not desire or associate with. Do as God say in Jer 29:1-9

Being invasive to challenges gives birth to skills.

Hidden skills and innovations usually manifest within communities of immigrants, because of the quest for survival. This is what crises or war, or famine are meant to bring out of us and not to destroy us. For instance, in America, survival of the fittest, invasive mentality is a great drive towards sustainability and wealth control.

The UK, during slave trades, America through arms, democracy, Nigerians, and the Chinese invading Africa with technology and infrastructures. The secrets to wealth and keys to destroying lack and famine are migration and invasiveness and not a destructive mentality mindset. If you are not invasive, you cannot win and cannot be rich. Be invasive in the space you find yourself.

To be invasive simply means, to have an attitude or nature that is not indigenous to a particular field, location, or idea. And so, to be invasive, you must adapt to new areas easily, you must reproduce quickly, and also be harmless this time to the natives and economy. Be invasive but be harmless. Seek the peace of the land. This is how to be successful and productive.

According to statistics, the remittance yearly by immigrants to their country of origin in many cases is more than the country's yearly budget.

Abraham, Isaac, and Jacob were all invasive but harmless. Do not be like the devil who invaded the garden of Eden and then destroyed Adam and Eve who were native to the garden. Be wise as a serpent and gentle as a dove. Do not apply wisdom that would destroy others. This is what Jesus Christ meant.

Goliath brought out the war skills in David. David was a shepherd before then. He was not even invited into the army of Israel for the war. But his gift manifested during the war. He was a great man of war and probably not a good king.

Anytime he is not at war front, he becomes restless and sinned against God. He prompted Joab to number Israel one time and God was angry with David. The other time he committed adultery. It Looks like any time that he was not at the war front, he found a way of bringing the war into his household or domain by sinning. You would be restless when you are not doing your purpose or calling.

If you are a man of prayer, when you are on vacation from prayer life, you become restless and commit sin or err against God.

Nigeria was in a civil war in the 1960s. This war revealed some skills and innovations that the country did not harness for her own good from all the tribes involved or who participated in the civil war (Igbos, Yorubas, and Hausas). The Igbos came up with different ammunition, technology, and mechanical war equipment made locally. The Yorubas are IT experts while the Hausas are political strategists. But the country failed to harness these skills to better the lots of the common man.

Cookies for Influence: Maintaining Power and Control

God created man in Genesis 1 to have power and control everything He created.

Do not empower a man to the point that they no longer need you. Always give room for continuous craving for your expertise or views on matters inspired by your personal growth and change of level.

When you give an idea or solution to a problem, ensure that you are still relevant in the execution of the idea or solution. Learn from Joseph and Pharaoh the king of Egypt.

Gen 41: 33 - 39

Now therefore let Pharaoh look out a man discreet and wise, and set him over the land of Egypt. Let Pharaoh do this, and let him appoint officers over the land, and take up the fifth part of the land of Egypt in the seven plenteous years. And let them gather all the food of those good years that come, and lay up corn under the hand of Pharaoh, and let them keep food in the cities. And that food shall be for store to the land against the seven years of famine, which shall be in the land of Egypt; that the land perish not through the famine. And the thing was good in the eyes of Pharaoh, and in the eyes of all his servants. And Pharaoh said unto his servants, Can we find such a one as this is, a man in whom the Spirit of God is? And Pharaoh said unto Joseph, Forasmuch as God hath shewed thee all this, there is none so discreet and wise as thou art:

Joseph and Daniel proffered solutions in their days. They managed the execution of their ideas and suggestions. Note, that AI or computer cannot be so empowered to the point that human contributions would no longer be needed. This is how the system is designed. It is still humans that would keep updating or improving the AI of computer systems.

The Devil felt empowered to the point that he thought he no longer needed God, he wanted to be like God. He is in trouble till today.

Eve wanted to be empowered to be like God, in other words, to no longer need God. The world is still in trouble today.

God's system is to empower humans, but not to the point or level where humans would no longer need Him to do their things. It is God's glory to conceal a matter.

Prov 25: 2

It is the glory of God to conceal a thing: but the honour of kings is to search out a matter.

Every vision of God or ideas from God is an empowerment. But you would need Him all the way to execute the ideas or vision.

Eccl 8: 6 - 7

Because to every purpose there is time and judgment, therefore the misery of man is great upon him. For he knoweth not that which shall be: for who can tell him when it shall be

Be wise but do not be wicked. Be wise as a serpent but gentle as a dove. We are not sufficient of ourselves, but our sufficiency is from God.

Matthew 10:16

Behold, I send you forth as sheep in the midst of wolves: be ye therefore wise as serpents, and harmless as doves.

God put seals on dreams, visions, etc, so that you keep consulting Him for understanding or interpretations. He then opens the seal's precepts by precepts. Which means you will always need Him.

Matthew 13: 10 - 13

And the disciples came, and said unto him, Why speakest thou unto them in parables? He answered and said unto them, Because it is given unto you to know the mysteries of the kingdom of heaven, but to them it is not given. For whosoever hath, to him shall be given, and he shall have more abundance: but whosoever hath not, from him shall be taken away even that he hath. Therefore speak I to them in parables: because they seeing see not; and hearing they hear not, neither do they understand.

Your love might be the needed reason for some to keep coming back or for someone to demonstrate that they still need you.

Some spouses get carried away by their empowerment and achievements, and they think they no longer need their partner. This is the reason a lot stagnated or become limited or even lost their lives or are placed under a curse or lose their place in destiny. Just like Judas who betrayed Jesus because he thought he no longer needs our Lord Jesus.

The root of all evil is when someone thinks he does not need you in their lives anymore. For anyone who would do you evil, must have concluded that he or she does not need you or no longer needs you.

Each time the Israelites think they are empowered and self-sufficient or that things are going great for them, they think they no longer need God. So they erred, God then punished them, they ran back to God for help, then went back again into errors and ran back again to God.

 This is how the system is run. No human would ever be self-sufficient, to the point that they would no longer need the help of God. Whatever they are, whether big men, wealthy or celebrities.

Do not ever give an idea anywhere, that anyone would find easy to execute without your involvement. If you must always stay relevant.

Your ideas supports or visions are your POWER and INFLUENCE, do not be careless with it. For the world will take it away without remembering you.

I once shared an idea with a group of friends in the university where I once worked. Then, one of them took the idea and co-opted another senior colleague and they presented the idea to the University management as theirs, hoping to cash out on it without our knowledge or involvement. When I heard about it, I simply told the rest of the group that they should be calm and that the guy's efforts would fail. Because I never shared an idea that would no longer need my contributions. What he stole was an incomplete or the simplest version of the original.

Also, I know a person who empowered a friend to achieve a higher degree. And as soon as the degree was obtained, the friend out of pride and arrogance saw the higher degree as an opportunity for an independent life. Thinking the helper was no longer needed and subjected the benefactor to emotional pain. It never ended well.

Friends, men cannot be trusted and are known for their use and dump attitude. If you want to move higher and far, please do not engage in a use-and-dump approach. Appreciate the people who have contributed to your success story. Even if you think, you no longer need them. For blessed is he that cometh in the name of the Lord.

I know a church and a minister, who after using the people to launch his ministry moved to another location, then felt he had arrived and neglected the people. That branch had problems due to that move and its growth suffered serious delays. Until thou said blessed is he that cometh in the name of the Lord, things might not go the right way.

This is the reason companies or manufacturers keep innovating, they do not want you to ever think, you no longer need them. They keep releasing yearly versions of improved software or cars, or devices. So whatever empowerment you already have is not eternally sufficient for your needs, it must become obsolete. Otherwise, they won't make money, otherwise they would go bankrupt.

Only the poor or the unwise would give it all without needing to return or recourse to them.

If you display wisdom, show, or demonstrate wisdom that makes you indispensable, not such that makes you feel that you are no longer needed or necessary like Ahithophel, then you will endure and become great.

Even nature is designed in this pattern. Rain performs its role in such a way that you keep needing it every year. There will never be a time that rain will no longer be needed if man lives on earth. So also, the sun, the moon, the land, and so on. They each make you keep desiring them and cultivating them. Just imagine if we are paying for these, how rich the sun, rain, and land would be by now, just doing their jobs and making themselves indispensable.

A thing is as important as how often people continuously go back to it or desire it. What makes something important is how often it is used or approached. That is the secret of pay per click pay per download or pay per view. If you want to be great and wealthy, you must be continuously desired and celebrated.

It is only the poor that gives all and no one goes back for more of them. If your idea is poor, no one returns for more. If your wisdom is poor or shallow, no one returns to you to hear more. Solomon's wisdom was extraordinary, so all over the world he had visitors who visited to hear his wisdom and gave him gifts. You soon run dry if no one continuously needs you in their lives.

Take note, anything that can bless or empower you, also can curse you. Anyone that can help you up, can also bring you down. For instance, Eve was Adam's helpmeet, she also brought Adam down with her. Also, consider a building elevator, it can take you up and down. However, not everything that can bring you down can also push you up. Consider a parachute for instance. So, be careful and strategic.

Jesus was set for the rise and fall of many in Israel. So also the office of prophets. Some will rise or fall through them, depending on how you relate to them.

Luke 2: 33 - 34

And Joseph and his mother marvelled at those things which were spoken of him. And Simeon blessed them, and said unto Mary his mother, Behold, this child is set for the fall and rising again of many in Israel; and for a sign which shall be spoken against;

During Moses' days, one Abihu and co thought they were now sufficient of themselves and that they no longer needed Moses. Whatever Moses was able to do, they felt they could do also. Forgetting that their empowerment was from Moses and because of Moses. Hence, they suffered for their foolishness.

The same mechanism that helped you to rise can also hold your downfall. If you have to be punished, the same power that God gives you to build people up can be used to destroy the same people too. Please tread softly.

2 Corinthians 13:10

Therefore I write these things being absent, lest being present I should use sharpness, according to the power which the Lord hath given me to edification, and not to destruction.

The challenge these days is that Christians now think they know everything, they have the Holy Spirit and so, they no longer need God in their affairs anymore. If the world knows how to keep your appetite desiring for more innovations. How much more our God. So, hear this, the death, resurrection of Jesus, and the gift of the Holy Spirit are not all that God can offer. He has much more and wants you to come craving more of Him. God is indispensable from generation to generation.

Cookies for Agelessness: Subduing the Effects of Day and Night

Man was ageless before the fall of Man. We were created in the likeness of God who is ageless. God gave man dominion over all He created including day and night. In the beginning, day and night never had negative effects on man. Though the man was on Earth, he was not subjected to the laws governing the earth. Meaning man never had to sleep because it was night or got tired because he exerted strength on any matter. Until man fell.

Genesis 1:28

And God blessed them, and God said unto them, Be fruitful, and multiply, and replenish the earth, and subdue it: and have dominion over the fish of the sea, and over the fowl of the air, and over every living thing that moveth upon the earth

One of the scriptures that shows clearly when God started subjecting man to the laws governing the earth is in

Genesis 8: 22

While the earth remaineth, seedtime and harvest, and cold and heat, and summer and winter, and day and night shall not cease.

When man fell in Eden, man had his days numbered because he now has an end which is death and so because of that, there must also be a beginning which was the time Adam and Eve fell. This is just as the existence of a man included the 9 months spent in the womb. But man's age starts counting the day he was or is born.

The age of Adam recorded in the Bible started from when he fell, not when he was created. Before man fell, age was not to be counted because death or the end of man was not in the picture at that time. This is how it is in heaven, with the angels, and with God too.

This is why, when man was formed, the Bible did not use the phrase ' and there was day and there was night because the man was not subjected to be ruled by day and night.

This grace was displayed by God in the wilderness when day and night did not affect the materials, shoes, and clothes and the body of Israelites never aged or worn out. They maintained their freshness throughout their journey in the wilderness.

Deuteronomy 29: 5 - 6

And I have led you forty years in the wilderness: your clothes are not waxen old upon you, and thy shoe is not waxen old upon thy foot. Ye have not eaten bread, neither have ye drunk wine or strong drink: that ye might know that I am the LORD your God

God was in a way showing man what they lost in the Garden of Eden. Man can forever remain fresh and young, be ageless, and not affected by day and night despite the use of their bodies or materials.

Caleb also testified to this grace, at 80 he was still with the strength and body of a 40-year-old.

Joshua 14: 10 - 12

And now, behold, the LORD hath kept me alive, as he said, these forty and five years, even since the LORD spake this word unto Moses, while the children of Israel wandered in the wilderness: and now, lo, I am this day fourscore and five years old. As yet I am as strong this day as I was in the day that Moses sent me: as my strength was then, even so is my strength now, for war, both to go out, and to come in. Now therefore give me this mountain, whereof the LORD spake in that day; for thou heardest in that day how the Anakims were there, and that the cities were great and fenced: if so be the LORD will be with me, then I shall be able to drive them out, as the LORD said.

You can be 100 years and your body is exactly 25 years old. Man can be ageless. Not affected by day and night or world diseases.

The sun shall not smite you by day nor the moon by night. Even though the sun and the moon can provide other good benefits, they can still reduce the well-being of man. They can also smite, strike, or kill. Do you remember that the moon and stars fought alongside Prophetess Deborah to defeat Sisera in Judges 5:20

Psalms 121:6 - 7

The sun shall not smite thee by day, nor the moon by night. The Lord shall preserve thee from all evil: He shall preserve thy soul.

This is not divine health. It is agelessness where your body and strength don't grow old or wear out or weak. When your body looks so much younger than your age.

Joshua commanded the sun to stand still. Because the Israelites were losing the battle or becoming weaker as the sun went down or as the night took over from the day. Because each time the day takes over from the night or the night takes over from the day, man loses strength or energy and becomes weaker or worn out.

For instance, if you are a man of the night, you are active in the night but in the day you are weak or lose strength and vice versa.

The point is that man never sleeps or slumbers before the fall of man. Because they were never exhausted, they did not need sleep. Just like angels and in the likeness of God who neither sleep nor slumber.

Before man fell, the man was without beginning and end. Just like the angels and God. Their existence was not numbered in days, nights, or years. The numbering of their days started counting right from the very moment that Adam and Eve fell.

Thy steadfast love of the Lord never changes, and His mercies never come to an end, they are new every morning.

Lamentation 3: 22 - 23

The steadfast love of the LORD never ceases; his mercies never come to an end; they are new every morning; great is your faithfulness.

To subdue the earth means to subdue everything that has control of the earth, or has influence on the earth's operations, which includes day and night, the moon, sun, and the stars. Whether natural, physical, or spiritual. Have full control of the earth, not the earth controlling or overwhelming man.

Cookies for Growth: Starting from the beginning

The book of Genesis 1 demonstrated how God patiently began all things from the beginning. By not skipping any process.

The process of harvesting starts with tilling the ground. Then planting, watering, waiting, cultivation, and then harvesting. No one builds a house without starting from the foundation.

Zachariah 4: 10

For who hath despised the day of small things? for they shall rejoice, and shall see the plummet in the hand of Zerubbabel with those seven; they are the eyes of the Lord, which run to and fro through the whole earth.

Please start from the beginning. Even Jesus was born a baby. Not from high positions among religious leaders or political leaders. Even at baptism, he subjected himself to the process and went through the first step to his greatness.

Abraham did not enter Canaan or Egypt as a prince, he went on to become a servant and grew to become great.

Genesis 24:1

And Abraham was old, and well stricken in age: and the LORD had blessed Abraham in all things.

I am not here to assume a high-flying position but to start from scratch and grow up to greatness. Joseph went to Egypt as a slave, the lowest status of life, and lived to become great. You may have to be a taxi driver first before you control a multi-million-dollar business.

God took me to South Africa. Started on the lowest status. Even with the lowest scholarship, while others were getting high-flier funding. But it took me about 4 to 5 years to start harvesting. I waited on God until He said it was my time.

Cookies for Opener: Law of First Thing First

To be successful, do the first thing first. You have to engage in what is most important in the order of things. In Genesis, God had a project in mind called MAN. But He took five days to create what was needed first. In any matter, there is always the first thing that must be done first to achieve success.

Gen 1:1 - 28

In the beginning God created the heaven and the earth. And the earth was without form, and void; and darkness was upon the face of the deep. And the Spirit of God moved upon the face of the waters. And God said, Let there be light: and there was light. And God saw the light, that it was good: and God divided the light from the darkness. And God called the light Day, and the darkness he called Night. And the evening and the morning were the first day…..

The one that goes first prepares the way for the success of others that are coming. Like John prepared the way ahead of Jesus. So, John the Baptist opened the salvation womb for Christ.

Mark 1: 3

The voice of one crying in the wilderness, Prepare ye the way of the Lord, make his paths straight.

Mark 9: 11

And they asked him, saying, Why say the scribes that Elias must first come?

Israel was going to war but enquired of the Lord and God said Judah must go first before other tribes to ensure victory.

Judges 20:18

And the children of Israel arose, and went up to the house of God, and asked counsel of God, and said, Which of us shall go up first to the battle against the children of Benjamin? And the LORD said Judah shall go up first.

As for me, South Africa was my first point of call in my journey outside my home country before my destination country for His plans for my life to be fulfilled. God did send people ahead of me that were ordained to meet my needs at each point in time.

For a great blessed home and generation, the firstborn must go in first. For God to give Canaan to his people, Abraham must go first into Canaan. For Israel to possess Canaan, they must be in slavery in Egypt first.

Genesis 15: 12 - 14

And when the sun was going down, a deep sleep fell upon Abram; and, lo, an horror of great darkness fell upon him. And he said unto Abram, Know of a surety that thy seed shall be a stranger in a land that is not theirs, and shall serve them; and they shall afflict them four hundred years; And also that nation, whom they shall serve, will I judge: and afterward

For Israel to be sold into slavery in Egypt, Joseph must go in first. If another of Jacob's sons had gone to Egypt as a slave first instead of Joseph, who would have interpreted Pharaoh's dream?, the vision would have failed. God knows how to order things.

For Israel to get out of slavery, Moses must be out of slavery first. Before he was able to bring the whole of Israel out.

To create a system of helpers and smooth progress, you must help the right person first. If you help the wrong person first, the vision will stall and fail. There is always the right person to help first to create a supply chain of helpers.

For a man to be subjected to sin, Adam and Eve must sin first. For God to save the world and mankind, Jesus must come first. That is why there must first be a fall away before the evil man, the antichrist is revealed.

2 Thessalonians 2:3

Let no man deceive you by any means: for that day shall not come, except there come a falling away first, and that man of sin be revealed, the son of perdition.

Have you ever seen a child born and just jump to high school without primary school? No, because primary school must come first.

Firstborns have the capacity to open the womb or break through it. If the right child opens the womb, it paves the way for other children to flow through. The first always opens the door: the first is an opener, a life starter.

To build a house you must do the first thing first by reaching out to the building team to give you the cost estimate of the structure.

Luke 14: 28 - 32

For which of you, intending to build a tower, sitteth not down first, and counteth the cost, whether he have sufficient to finish it? Lest haply, after he hath laid the foundation, and is not able to finish it, all that behold it begin to mock him, Saying, This man began to build, and was not able to finish. Or what king, going to make war against another king, sitteth not down first, and consulteth whether he be able with ten thousand to meet him that cometh against him with twenty thousand? Or else, while the other is yet a great way off, he sendeth an ambassage, and desireth conditions of peace.

Before Jesus could start his ministry, John the Baptist must go first or must start first. Before Jesus would baptize others, he must first be baptized by John and with water.

The first thing must be done first to fulfill all righteousness. To break through, you have to fulfill all righteousness. That is, do the first thing first.

Matthew 3: 13 - 15

Then cometh Jesus from Galilee to Jordan unto John, to be baptized of him. But John forbad him, saying, I have need to be baptized of thee, and comest thou to me? And Jesus answering said unto him, Suffer it to be so now: for thus it becometh us to fulfil all righteousness. Then he suffered him.

Seek first the kingdom of heaven, then other things shall be added.

Matthew 6: 33

But seek ye first the kingdom of God, and his righteousness; and all these things shall be added unto you.

The first always has the capacity and ability to create a smooth passage for others who are willing to follow suit. The first can ensure progressions. It can create a progressive environment or system and the ability to create a sustainable growth path.

You want to start a ministry: seek the first person first (the first convert first), that would pave the way for others. Do you want to start a music ministry? Seek the first person first, who would help propagate your music. If you want to start a business, to succeed, seek the first client first, that will announce your business to the whole world. It is a mystery until the first touches it, no success is guaranteed.

The first disciples that Jesus got were the ones who brought others to Jesus (John 1:35-51). You need fruitful disciples, seek the right person first. Seek the first step first in all things.

The law of first thing first, made Jesus create his ministry around the disciples not around his families and friends. This is why the church is lasting till today. Those ministries created around families and friends would likely not go beyond three generations. But the church is still standing now.

Jesus started ministry with no families and friends. It was entirely with total strangers, who were ordained by God to be engines and the propellers of the vision Jesus had.

If Jesus were to be married, he would still have embarked on his vision without the wife. Little wonder apostle Peter's wife was not involved in all the ministry of Jesus. We only heard of Mary and Martha. Didn't you notice that none of David's family was with him throughout the trouble he encountered? Other tribes gave David their full support. Only for Judah to show up later when David had already won the battle. You must seek to have the first person or people or seek to see or know the first step in whatever you are embarking on. Even in business, stop looking for friends and family structures. Seek the first right ones or people that the vision or business had ordained to be part of it or ordained to help propel it.

Cookies for wisdom: Seeking Knowledge and Understanding as SILVER

In every situation, there is a lot of knowledge hidden and understanding that we lack. Because every matter is concealed, and we must seek God to unseal the package. It is the will of God that we know about what is happening around us and gain an understanding of the way out and solutions. For this is wisdom passed to us through the instructions that God releases to us.

Prov 2: 3 - 6

Yea, if thou criest after knowledge, and liftest up thy voice for understanding; If thou seekest her as silver, and searchest for her as for hid treasures; Then shalt thou understand the fear of the LORD, and find the knowledge of God. For the LORD giveth wisdom: out of his mouth cometh knowledge and understanding.

For God to speak, we must seek knowledge regarding all issues we go through and raise our voices to gain understanding with all our hearts. Seek it the way you seek silver (treasure or money). We must seek it with all our hearts and then we shall find him.

Jeremiah 29:13

And ye shall seek me, and find me, when ye shall search for me with all your heart.

For you to transact successfully in the kingdom, knowledge and understanding are the silver you must spend in exchange for wealth and glory. They are your spending power to enjoy plenty and success.

And then from the mouth of the Lord shall come forth wisdom, knowledge, and understanding to instruct you in the way you should go to have success.

Prov 4: 5 - 9

Get wisdom, get understanding: forget it not; neither decline from the words of my mouth. Forsake her not, and she shall preserve thee: love her, and she shall keep thee. Wisdom is the principal thing; therefore get wisdom: and with all thy getting, get understanding. Exalt her, and she shall promote thee: she shall bring thee to honour, when thou dost embrace her. She shall give to thine head an ornament of grace: a crown of glory shall she deliver to thee.

Let your heart crave it, crave it as if your life depends on it. The currency you spend in exchange for success or to ensure victories is knowledge and understanding. In all things get wisdom and in all thy getting, get understanding. Getting the understanding of all thy getting. The how and when, or what or why you're getting a thing must be searched out. Many things that we pass through have understandings and instructions attached to them.

Jesus admonished us.

The kingdom of God flourishes through instructions from the mouth of God

Asking questions to gain knowledge and understanding on any matter is the key to wisdom.

Be wise as a serpent: the serpent came to Eve asking what the Lord said.

The serpent asked God does Job serve you for nothing. Trying to gain understanding and knowledge. And God gave the Devil knowledge and instructions because the Devil sought for it.

Prov 24: 14

So shall the knowledge of wisdom be unto thy soul; when thou hast found it, then there shall be a reward, and thy expectation shall not be cut off.

Be wise, seek knowledge.

Cookies for wisdom: Serve to Preserve and Prolong Your Life

Do the work of the ministry, and never confuse service with ministry. Ministry is not what you get out of service but what you put in, in service. It's about the state of mind when serving. For ministry to be right before God, the intent must be right and perfect in honor and fear of God. Service to God or our labor of love, is serving God not as in a merchandising mindset but serving without the feeling of trading, or entitlement for a payback or reward. Not eye service and not for the praise from men.

Matthew 6: 5

And when thou prayest, thou shalt not be as the hypocrites are: for they love to pray standing in the synagogues and in the corners of the streets, that they may be seen of men. Verily I say unto you, They have their reward.

That is, if God blesses you or not, you will still commit yourself to service without looking back.

Habakkuk 3: 17 - 18

Although the fig tree shall not blossom, Neither shall fruit be in the vines;

The labour of the olive shall fail, And the fields shall yield no meat; The flock shall be cut off from the fold, And there shall be no herd in the stalls:

Yet I will rejoice in the LORD, I will joy in the God of my salvation.

If you give your alms or offerings, give as serving not as a businessman expecting returns of profit. If you pray, worship, love, do so serving not with the mind of being blessed in return or you stop serving your attitudes.

Nothing shall separate us from the love of God….not death, love, hate, sex, good, bad…

Romans 8: 35 - 39

Who shall separate us from the love of Christ? shall tribulation, or distress, or persecution, or famine, or nakedness, or peril, or sword? As it is written, For thy sake we are killed all the day long; we are accounted as sheep for the slaughter. Nay, in all these things we are more than conquerors through him that loved us. For I am persuaded that neither death, nor life, nor angels, nor principalities, nor powers, nor things present, nor things to come, Nor height, nor depth, nor any other creature, shall be able to separate us from the love of God, which is in Christ Jesus our Lord.

True service is a great tool to have your life preserved and prolonged whenever you need intervention in the face of life-threatening challenges.

2 Kings 20: 1 - 6

In those days was Hezekiah sick unto death. And the prophet Isaiah the son of Amoz came to him, and said unto him, Thus saith the Lord, Set thine house in order; for thou shalt die, and not live. Then he turned his face to the wall, and prayed unto the Lord, saying, I beseech thee, O Lord, remember now how I have walked before thee in truth and with a perfect heart, and have done that which is good in thy sight. And Hezekiah wept sore. And it came to pass, afore Isaiah was gone out into the middle court, that the word of the Lord came to him, saying, Turn again, and tell Hezekiah the captain of my people, Thus saith the Lord, the God of David thy father, I have heard thy prayer, I have seen thy tears: behold, I will heal thee: on the third day thou shalt go up unto the house of the Lord. And I will add unto thy days fifteen years; and I will deliver thee and this city out of the hand of the king of Assyria; and I will defend this city for mine own sake, and for my servant David's sake.

Hezekiah prayed to the Lord to remember how he served Him! That is, in tithes, in giving of alms to the poor and needy, in offerings and sacrifices, in helping the widows and orphans and the sick or less privileged.

Did God forget those services rendered by Hezekiah? Nay. For God does not forget our labor of love.

Hebrew 6: 10

For God is not unrighteous so as to forget your work and labor of love, which ye have shown toward His name, in that ye have ministered to the saints, and do minister.

Just like Hezekiah if you are confident that you genuinely served Him, you can raise the issue. Since Hezekiah raised the issue, God must protect His integrity, for no one serves Him for nothing. The reward for service is not what you demand but what you must earn.

I have a good friend who twice in the face of life-threatening illnesses presented his resume of service like Hezekiah to God. And God rewarded him by raising him from his bed of languishing in no time even to the doctor's surprise.

The devil asked God, does Job serve you for nothing?

Job 1: 9

Then Satan answered the Lord, and said, Doth Job fear God for nought?

God said I have not asked the seed of Jacob to serve me in vain.

Isaiah 45: 19

I have not spoken in secret, in a dark place of the earth; I said not unto the seed of Jacob, 'Seek ye Me in vain.' I, the Lord, speak righteousness; I declare things that are right.

Hezekiah got an extension of 15 years extra to his life.

2 Kings 20:6

And I will add unto thy days fifteen years; and I will deliver thee and this city out of the hand of the king of Assyria; and I will defend this city for mine own sake, and for my servant David's sake.

The devil meant to kill Job until God said Job's life must not be touched.

Job 1:12

And the Lord said unto Satan, Behold, all that he hath is in thy power; only upon himself put not forth thine hand. So Satan went forth from the presence of the Lord.

Can you imagine that after the trial of Job, Job later gave birth to 7 sons and 3 daughters, who were the most beautiful maidens of their days?

Job 42: 12 - 15

So the Lord blessed the latter end of Job more than his beginning: for he had fourteen thousand sheep, and six thousand camels, and a thousand yoke of oxen, and a thousand she asses. He had also seven sons and three daughters. And he called the name of the first, Jemima; and the name of the second, Kezia; and the name of the third, Kerenhappuch. And in all the land were no women found so fair as the daughters of Job: and their father gave them inheritance among their brethren.

Now, let's calculate, assuming there were 2 years of space in between the children. So, there would be roughly 20 years after the devil's attack on Job for the birth of the 10 children Job later had. And also, for the beauty of the women to be seen and notable, the children would have to be at least 18 years of age. In other words, Job must have enjoyed an extra 30-year extension to his life from the time of the attack. All because of genuine service.

Stop praying for bread and butter. Your Father in heaven knows your needs. Stop reminding God about your service anytime you need a house, car, or material things. It is a waste of grace and the treasure stored for you in heaven.

Matthew 6: 7 - 8

But when ye pray, use not vain repetitions, as the heathen do: for they think that they shall be heard for their much speaking. Be not ye therefore like unto them: for your

Father knoweth what things ye have need of, before ye ask him.

Matthew 6: 19 - 21

Lay not up for yourselves treasures upon earth, where moth and rust doth corrupt, and where thieves break through and steal: but lay up for yourselves treasures in heaven, where neither moth nor rust doth corrupt, and where thieves do not break through nor steal: for where your treasure is, there will your heart be also.

Jesus said, your life is worth much more than raiment. Raise the issue of service only when your life is under threat, when death comes knocking, when terminal diseases show up and God can then use your earned reward for service to grant you an extra 15 - 40 years to your life.

Matthew 6: 25

Therefore I say unto you, Take no thought for your life, what ye shall eat, or what ye shall drink; nor yet for your body, what ye shall put on. Is not the life more than meat, and the body than raiment?

God will put a mark of difference between those who served Him and those who served Him not.

Malachi 3: 18

Then you will again see the difference between the righteous and the wicked, between those who serve God and those who do not."

God cannot be deceived; He knows those who are His

2 Timothy 2:19

Nevertheless the foundation of God standeth sure, having this seal, The Lord knoweth them that are his. And, Let everyone that nameth the name of Christ depart from iniquity.

Nahum 1: 7

The Lord is good, a stronghold in the day of trouble, and he knoweth them that trust in him

For the dead can no longer serve or praise Him. That was what Hezekiah called God's attention to when his life was under severe threat.

Isaiah 38: 18 - 20

For the grave cannot praise thee, death cannot celebrate thee: They that go down into the pit cannot hope for thy truth. The living, the living, he shall praise thee, as I do this day: The father to the children shall make known thy truth. The LORD was ready to save me: Therefore we will sing my songs to the stringed instruments. All the days of our life in the house of the LORD.

Service is an assured and guaranteed way to secure an extension to your life that is facing truncation.

In the book of Acts, a woman called Dorcas died, apostle Peter was told of her great works towards the saints and the church. Peter had to raise her back to life.

Cookies for wisdom: Faith Without Counting the Costs

Everything has costs, but it was not for you to bear. When he sent them, they lacked nothing. We have allowed so many earthly principles to interfere with our relationship and knowledge of God.

Luke 22: 35

And he said unto them, When I sent you without purse, and scrip, and shoes, lacked ye any thing? And they said, Nothing.

I have never in my life seen a clearer picture before taking a leap of faith. I have never counted the cost of my actions as ordered by the Lord, because I am not the builder or financier. Christ is the builder, he only brought me into the house he already built. So Christ counts the costs, not me. He counts and knows the costs of choosing me and the assignment.

John 14: 2

In my Father's house are many mansions: if it were not so, I would have told you. I go to prepare a place for you.

When Jesus said, I go to prepare a place for you! The responsibility lies on him to count the costs, not me. The cost that I have to count is that of following him. I cannot look back when my hands are already on the plough.

Luke 9: 62

And Jesus said unto him, No man, having put his hand to the plough, and looking back, is fit for the kingdom of God.

Because Abram does not want to be counting the costs of anything he looked for the city which has a foundation whose maker and builder is God.

Hebrew 11: 8 - 10

By faith Abraham, when he was called to go out into a place which he should after receive for an inheritance, obeyed; and he went out, not knowing whither he went. By faith he sojourned in the land of promise, as in a strange country, dwelling in tabernacles with Isaac and Jacob, the heirs with him of the same promise: For he looked for a city which hath foundations, whose builder and maker is God.

So, he was not considering the implications because there was no cost for him to bear.

I have never in any stage taken any steps with a clear picture in view. I just take the step God counsels me to take. So I do not worry what the cost is. If I have any interest, I only pray about the interest, not the cost. And if God grants me support and counsel regarding the matter, I just move into action because His support means He is bearing the costs.

If God leads, instructs, or supports your interest, the cost implications are on Him, not you. So, stop counting the costs and focus only on Him. Have you ever wondered how Noah paid for the nails and the planks that were used in building the Ark? Because the money or cost was not his responsibility.

The only cost you must bear is that of believing in Him as I said. Whether He saved you or not, you have no room for regrets. These were the mindsets of the three Hebrew men.

Daniel 3: 16 - 18

Shadrach, Meshach, and Abednego, answered and said to the king, O Nebuchadnezzar, we are not careful to answer thee in this matter. If it be so, our God whom we serve is able to deliver us from the burning fiery furnace, and he will deliver us out of thine hand, O king. But if not, be it known unto thee, O king, that we will not serve thy gods, nor worship the golden image which thou hast set up.

One day I cried to God, saying Lord, you have given me a vision greater than my income or financial capacity. God said unto me, I never gave you a vision or dream or assignment that you would have to bear the costs. Since that time, I have reset my mind. God never gives visions based on your financial capacity, friend. Because the financial costs or the resources required for any vision are not yours to bear. The cost of any vision is on Him.

Apostle Ananias was instructed to meet with Saul (Paul), fear gripped him when he counted the costs of meeting with the man popularly known for killing the followers of Jesus. Christ had to dispel the fear, letting him know that the cost of his meeting with Saul was already paid by Him.

Acts 9: 10 - 16

And there was a certain disciple at Damascus, named Ananias; and to him said the Lord in a vision, Ananias. And he said, Behold, I am here, Lord. And the Lord said unto him, Arise, and go into the street which is called Straight, and inquire in the house of Judas for one called Saul, of Tarsus: for, behold, he prayeth, And hath seen in a vision a man named Ananias coming in, and putting his hand on him, that he might receive his sight. Then Ananias answered, Lord, I have heard by many of this man, how much evil he hath done to thy saints at Jerusalem: And here he hath authority from the chief priests to bind all that call on thy name. But the Lord said unto him, Go thy way: for he is a chosen vessel unto me, to bear my name before the Gentiles, and kings, and the children of Israel:

Have a cost but do not count the cost rely on God. Live like Abraham, who is the father of faith. Before Abraham, no one could figure it out that God can raise the dead. But when he was tempted to sacrifice Isaac, his spirit was enlightened and so the cost of sacrificing Isaac did not trouble him.

Hebrews 11: 17 - 19

By faith Abraham, when he was tried, offered up Isaac: and he that had received the promises offered up his only begotten son, Of whom it was said, That in Isaac shall thy seed be called: Accounting that God was able to raise him up, even from the dead; from whence also he received him in a figure.

Cookies for wisdom: Use LOVE as Your Ammunition

You can use faith to move mountains, but LOVE is what you need to protect and preserve yourself. Your love has more impact on your neighbors than your great faith. The only power connecting you to your neighbors is your love, not your faith. This is why the Bible says to love your neighbor as yourself.

1 Corinthians 13: 13

And now abide faith, hope, love, these three; but the greatest of these is love.

Unfortunately, we have many FAITH preachers today and little or no preachers of LOVE. This is why we have so many sick and weak believers in the body of Christ today in the presence of great faith. Because, they know how to only fight the fight of faith, and do not know that the fight of love and fight out of love is what heals, protects and preserves them and their society. Friend, love remains the greatest of these three. When you give, give out of love not in fear and when you fear, you have no reward. Don't give because you fear being harmed by the witches or wizards in your family if you do not give them. You won't have rewards for such giving and you would eventually end up in their belly. When you exercise faith, express your faith in love.

Ephesians 3: 18 - 20

may be able to comprehend with all saints what is the breadth, and length, and depth, and height; and to know the love of Christ, which passeth knowledge, that ye might be filled with all the fulness of God. Now unto him that can do exceeding abundantly above all that we ask or think, according to the power that worketh in us,

The love of Christ outweighs knowledge, it is what makes you to be filled with ALL the FULLNESS of God. Faith or hope cannot fill you up with God's fullness. Just imagine having the fullness of God in you. Do you think any harm can just come to you?

Give or fight in love and the God who is love and dwells in love will preserve and protect you and all that is yours. Love is powerful. Make sure love is the reason why you are giving, forgiving, serving, resisting, acting in faith, hoping, contending, or fighting. Fight to save not to destroy. This can only be achieved in love.

Hebrew 12: 5 - 7

And ye have forgotten the exhortation which speaketh unto you as unto children, My son, despise not thou the chastening of the Lord, nor faint when thou art rebuked of him: For whom the Lord loveth he chasteneth, and scourgeth every son whom he receiveth. If ye endure chastening, God dealeth with you as with sons; for what son is he whom the father chasteneth not?

The only reason God chastises is love. If you have to discipline or have to correct, do so in love.

Fight with a pure heart, not with hatred or envy. Fighting out of love saves souls. If any perish it will only be the child of perdition, the one destined to be so. Jesus showed Judas love, but his love was unable to save Judas.

John 17: 12

While I was with them in the world, I kept them in thy name: those that thou gavest me I have kept, and none of them is lost, but the son of perdition; that the scripture might be fulfilled.

There is no potent weapon that is as powerful as a pure heart in everything you do.

Psalms 51:10

Create in me a clean heart, O God; And renew a right spirit within me.

Do not fight like unbelievers or evil people. When they fight you, they think you are like them. They fight in the flesh, full of hatred, envy, and evil. If you contend with them with such minds, you will lose the battle and probably get destroyed.

Our weapons of warfare are not carnal. It is the weapons clothed with love that can pull down strongholds.

2 Corinthians 10:4

for the weapons of our warfare are not carnal, but mighty through God to the pulling down of strong holds;

When Jesus flogged and chased the Pharisees out of the temple, it was out of love. When he said Father forgive them, for they know not what they, it was out of love.

I have over the years learned not to embark on any contention without the end goal of saving the individual soul. Even if they have to go through afflictions and pains, it is for the salvation of their soul.

The Apostle Paul said we should hand over some individuals to the devil to be tormented so that their souls can be saved. In every contention let salvation be your utmost goal.

1 Corinthians 5:5

To deliver such an one unto Satan for the destruction of the flesh, that the spirit may be saved in the day of the Lord Jesus.

If it is not going to lead to saving a soul or so that the individual becomes a better and acceptable person in the sight of God. Do not be involved.

Do not be a friend of my enemy, is my enemy kind of person. Or the enemy of my friend is my enemy. Do not also be the enemy of my enemy, is my friend kind of a person. These minds would weaken your spiritual strength.

Never coarse anyone to join you to dislike anyone that you feel you don't like. God hates these things. Because your righteousness must exceed the righteousness of the Pharisees.

Matthew 5: 20

For I say unto you, That except your righteousness shall exceed the righteousness of the scribes and Pharisees, ye shall in no case enter into the kingdom of heaven.

In all battles or challenges that I have been faced with, I have always sought God's approval by letting Him know my intent and what I aimed at getting as the result. So, if my heart is pure and it pleases the Lord, He joins forces with me to achieve the goal. The devil provided a justifiable reason why Job must be tried, and so God permitted it. So also, be wise.

Therefore, in contention, the individual thinks he is fighting me or the flesh, not knowing he or she is fighting with God ultimately. For instance, for the salvation of

Israel God and Moses kept contending with Pharaoh using different techniques and afflictions. Pharaoh thought he was dealing with Moses, not knowing that he was contending with his maker. He underestimated Moses.

Your best secret to victory is to always ensure that your enemies underestimate you and your strength. Because if they can predict you correctly, they will win the battle. God did not intend that the enemies accurately estimate our worth or strength. They cannot even predict what we plan to do next. Our next move is always hidden.

This is what Jesus meant when he said they that are born of the spirit are like wind whose direction cannot be predicted.

John 3: 6 - 8

That which is born of the flesh is flesh; and that which is born of the Spirit is spirit. Marvel not that I said unto thee, Ye must be born again. The wind bloweth where it listeth, and thou hearest the sound thereof, but canst not tell whence it cometh, and whither it goeth: so is every one that is born of the Spirit.

For love, God allowed the devil to torment Job for the salvation of Job, not to destroy Job. The devil's sole aim was to destroy Job and he managed to get God's support to afflict the man of God. But God permitted the devil for the salvation of Job's soul. Because in all the afflictions Job did not curse God. God won in the end because He contended for and with Job out of love.

Throughout all of this, Job did not sin by what he said.

Job 2: 9 - 10

Then his wife told him, "Do you remain firm in your integrity? Curse God and die!" But he replied to her, "You're talking like foolish women do. Are we to accept what is good from God but not tragedy?"

The devil underestimated Job. It is only through love; you can turn what the enemies meant for evil for your good. Joseph's brothers contended with him with hatred and envy, but Joseph maintained love as his ammunition. The brothers indeed underestimated him. This is what happens when you fight your battles full of hatred and carnality. You would never be able to estimate your enemy's strength correctly.

Genesis 50:20

But as for you, ye thought evil against me; but God meant it unto good, to bring to pass, as it is this day, to save many people alive.

Whatever you do, do not do it for the wrong reasons. Do not pray, worship, or give or fight for wrong reasons. We would always lose if our motives were wrong.

Be careful also, so that what you started with love won't end up in envy and hatred. When you chastise or you are chastised, receive your chastisement in love. Not in anger or bitterness.

It's not easy, it's hard when you see yourself, your loved ones, your neighbors, or even your enemies passing through or being tried by fire. Let love's expected results be your joy. For all shall be to the praise, honor, and glory of Jesus Christ.

Jesus did not go through the cross for pride, or show of power, or for any selfish reason. But for LOVE. In all his confrontations, contention, and affliction, he was saved until his time. Because he faced all these challenges with LOVE. Despite His many oppositions both from the religious leaders and ordinary men who hated Him, His doctrines, and works without a cause He still LOVED them and did till His very end.

"Love looks through a telescope; envy (hatred, strife, bitterness, clamor, jealousy, anger, wrath, resentment, offense, and the likes) looks through a microscope." - Josh Billings (emphasis mine)

The goal of our faith is the salvation of souls.

Cookies for wisdom: One Step at a Time

One step at a time and ensure that the first step or system can sustain itself or run on its own without any further efforts from you. Do not be a jack of all trades and master of none.

Genesis 1: 1 - 12

….And the earth brought forth grass, and herb yielding seed after his kind, and the tree yielding fruit, whose seed was in itself, after his kind: and God saw that it was good….

God focused on a specific or matter per day, then waited to observe and confirm that everything was good. That is, everything was running and could sustain their activities without needing Him to do anything further to make it work. Once that was achieved, He then moved to add more activities or businesses.

Genesis 1: 13 - 27

….And God set them in the firmament of the heaven to give light upon the earth, And to rule over the day and over the night, and to divide the light from the darkness: and God saw that it was good….

God focused on specific projects per day and nourished until the project or system can run on its own continuously and sustain its operations. Then God concluded "It was good" and so moved to do something else. This is wisdom. If God had wanted to create all things at once or in a day, He had the power.

Luke 1: 35 - 37

The angel replied, "The Holy Spirit will come upon you, and the power of the Most High will overshadow you. So the Holy One to be born will be called the Son of God. Look, even Elizabeth your relative has conceived a son in her old age, and she who was called barren is in her sixth month. For no word from God will ever fail.

God had to wait until Elizabeth's pregnancy was 6 months and He noted it was good. He then proceeded to initiate Mary's divine assignment. One step at a time principle.

Ecclesiastes 8:6

Because to every purpose there is time and judgment, therefore the misery of man is great upon him.

Yes, everything has its procedures and its time. So be patient to allow the time to run its full course.

Cookies for wisdom: Do not live by emotions, live by the word of God

God would always test your loyalty to Him and His word with emotional events to see which of these influences you. Your emotional attachment to blood relations, to friends, or your submission to His word.

Abraham in Isaac's case was tried by God.

Genesis 22: 1 - 3

And it came to pass after these things, that God did tempt Abraham, and said unto him, Abraham: and he said, Behold, here I am. And he said, Take now thy son, thine only son Isaac, whom thou lovest, and get thee into the land of Moriah; and offer him there for a burnt offering upon one of the mountains which I will tell thee of. And Abraham rose up early in the morning, and saddled his ass, and took two of his young men with him, and Isaac his son, and clave the wood for the burnt offering, and rose up, and went unto the place of which God had told him.

Eli decided to ignore the law of God because the problem had to do with his children and because of that, Eli dishonored God. Eli failed the test. For God had commanded that any man who defiled His temple, the offerings and sacrifices be killed but Eli allowed emotional attachment to destroy him and his children. If the sins were committed by outsiders, Eli would not have hesitated to apply the law as commanded.

1 Samuel 2: 30

Wherefore the LORD God of Israel saith, I said indeed that thy house, and the house of thy father, should walk before me for ever: but now the LORD saith, Be it far from me; for them that honour me I will honour, and they that despise me shall be lightly esteemed.

1 Samuel 3: 13 - 14

For I have told him that I will judge his house for ever for the iniquity which he knoweth; because his sons made themselves vile, and he restrained them not. And therefore I have sworn unto the house of Eli, that the iniquity of Eli's house shall not be purged with sacrifice nor offering for ever.

There was also a similar occurrence involving King David's children. One raped his younger sister and two years after David did nothing to punish his erred son as commanded by the law of God. Emotions denied him his complete submission to the word of God.

2 Samuel 13: 10 - 14

And Amnon said unto Tamar, Bring the meat into the chamber, that I may eat of thine hand. And Tamar took the cakes which she had made, and brought them into the chamber to Amnon her brother. And when she had brought them unto him to eat, he took hold of her, and said unto her, Come lie with me, my sister. And she answered him, Nay, my brother, do not force me; for no such thing ought to be done in Israel: do not thou this folly. And I, whither shall I cause my shame to go? and as for thee, thou shalt be as one of the fools in Israel. Now therefore, I pray thee, speak unto the king; for he will not withhold me from thee. Howbeit he would not hearken unto her voice: but, being stronger than she, forced her, and lay with her

For anyone who raped a maiden, the Lord commanded that such a person be slain. It would have been easy to implement, if the issue had not been related to David, it would have been a smooth ride for David. Emotions and submission to emotions deprived saints of their God's lifting to higher spiritual heights.

There was a story involving Saul, his son Jonathan, and David, that is worth looking into. Jonathan knew that God had departed from his father Saul and that David was then the choice of God. But emotional attachment won't allow Jonathan to stay away from Saul. He was with Saul everywhere to fight alongside Saul in wars despite knowing that the man was already rejected. Unfortunately, Jonathan's life ended with Saul.

1 Samuel 20: 30 - 31

Then Saul's anger was kindled against Jonathan, and he said unto him, Thou son of the perverse rebellious woman, do not I know that thou hast chosen the son of Jesse to thine own confusion, and unto the confusion of thy mother's nakedness? For as long as the son of Jesse liveth upon the ground, thou shalt not be established, nor thy kingdom. Wherefore now send and fetch him unto me, for he shall surely die.

2 Samuel 1: 17 - 19

And David lamented with this lamentation over Saul and over Jonathan his son: (Also he bade them teach the children of Judah the use of the bow: behold, it is written in the book of Jasher.) The beauty of Israel is slain upon thy high places: how are the mighty fallen!

Jonathan perished because he allowed emotions to rule him instead of the word of God. He should have pitched his tent with David, whose side the Lord was on. His emotions toward the members of his household became the enemy that destroyed him.

Jesus said a man's enemy is the members of his household. Because emotional attachment with them can cause you to sin against God.

Matthew 10: 35 - 36

For I am come to set a man at variance against his father, and the daughter against her mother, and the daughter in law against her mother-in-law. And a man's foes shall be they of his own household.

Jesus said he who wants to follow me must forsake his brothers, sisters, and parents because emotional influence is as dangerous as idolatry. Because most times it makes you disobey or bend the truth and the word of God.

God is not a respecter of persons. Emotions can make you respect a person while at the same time dishonoring God. Jesus wrapped it up by saying my mother and father and brothers and sisters are they that do the will of God. Simply to say emotions have no place in the kingdom of God.

Matthew 12: 46 - 50

While he yet talked to the people, behold, his mother and his brethren stood without, desiring to speak with him. Then one said unto him, Behold, thy mother and thy brethren stand without, desiring to speak with thee. But he answered and said unto him that told him, Who is my mother? and who are my brethren? And he stretched forth his hand toward his disciples, and said, Behold my mother and my brethren! For whosoever shall do the will of my Father which is in heaven, the same is my brother, and sister, and mother.

The day you overcome being subjected to emotions but rather to the word of God is when you actually secure your ticket to supernatural experience with God and so, you can be relied upon and worthy to speak on God's behalf

Cookies for wisdom: Vision is Generational

What is revealed to us is given to us and our children.

Deuteronomy 29: 19

The secret things belong unto the LORD our God: but those things which are revealed belong unto us and to our children forever, that we may do all the words of this law.

When God gives a vision or a promise, to our fathers or mothers or you, it is for you and your generation. Whatever or whichever part of the Vision, that you couldn't fulfill, God visits your next generation to show them the vision or covenant He had with their fathers for them to pursue it.

Genesis 26: 1 - 5

And there was a famine in the land, beside the first famine that was in the days of Abraham. And Isaac went unto Abimelech king of the Philistines unto Gerar. And the LORD appeared unto him, and said, Go not down into Egypt; dwell in the land which I shall tell thee of: Sojourn in this land, and I will be with thee, and will bless thee; for unto thee, and unto thy seed, I will give all these countries, and I will perform the oath which I sware unto Abraham thy father; And I will make thy seed to multiply as the stars of heaven, and will give unto thy seed all these countries; and in thy seed shall all the nations of the earth be blessed; Because that Abraham obeyed my voice, and kept my charge, my commandments, my statutes, and my laws.

So from generation to generation, He keeps transferring the vision to your downline because that vision is already given to you and your generation to fulfill.

Genesis 28: 13 - 15

And, behold, the LORD stood above it, and said, I am the LORD God of Abraham thy father, and the God of Isaac: the land whereon thou liest, to thee will I give it, and to thy seed; And thy seed shall be as the dust of the earth, and thou shalt spread abroad to the west, and to the east, and to the north, and to the south: and in thee and in thy seed shall all the families of the earth be blessed. And, behold, I am with thee, and will keep thee in all places whither thou goest, and will bring thee again into this land; for I will not leave thee, until I have done that which I have spoken to thee of.

This is why God kept visiting the Israelites showing them the covenant He had with Abraham and what they had to do.

God showed me a covenant He had with my grandfather in terms of riches and wealth through trading (sales) business in righteousness. Meaning the wealth will last as long in the hands of the one that is righteous in business or truthful in business.

If God gives you a vision, accept it and believe. It will be yours and that of your descendants if they are found worthy before God.

If you fulfill it, then enjoy it in righteousness. If you for any reason are unable to see it fulfilled in your lifetime, God preserves or reserves the vision for your descendants to fulfill.

Genesis 15: 13 - 16

And he said unto Abram, Know of a surety that thy seed shall be a stranger in a land that is not theirs, and shall serve them; and they shall afflict them four hundred years; And also that nation, whom they shall serve, will I judge: and afterward shall they come out with great substance. And thou shalt go to thy fathers in peace; thou shalt be buried in a good old age. But in the fourth generation they shall come hither again: for the iniquity of the Amorites is not yet full.

God on several occasions told Abraham that the vision of Canaan will be fulfilled by his descendants. The same thing happened to David. David had a vision to build a temple for God. But God chose Solomon to build the temple or fulfill the vision.

1 King 8: 18 - 19

And the LORD said unto David my father, Whereas it was in thine heart to build an house unto my name, thou didst well that it was in thine heart. Nevertheless thou shalt not build the house; but thy son that shall come forth out of thy loins, he shall build the house unto my name.

Therefore, no vision is lost, wasted, or unused if it is received and nurtured by faith and hope. If you look around you, you will see many old or living musicians having their descendants following in their footsteps. So also, the descendants of some general overseers are doing the same and actors and actresses all have their descendants having a representation in the industry of the uplines.

Why? Because it does not matter whether you are a believer or unbeliever, a vision stays and belongs to whosoever received it.

Before I moved to the US, my father, mother, grandfather, or grandmother must have received the vision. But they didn't know what or comprehend the city or time of fulfillment. But when it was time, I was on a visit to the US when God visited me in a vision saying "I still want you here". So, later I was wondering, when did God ever talk to me about relocating to the US? You see, it must have been received by one of my upline or grandparents. And God was just relating with me with the vision to get it fulfilled.

Friend, vision is generational. So stop praying only against generational curses but rather channel your strength to pray for the fulfillment of generational visions and blessings. For God is capable of transferring the wealth of many generations to you.

Little wonder the Bible says the gift and the callings of God are without repentance. Because once given and received, the gifts and callings or visions eternally remain yours and that of your children's children.

Most times what we call generational curses are shields or seals or veils that have blindfolded us, thereby causing us to turn our eyes away from generational blessings and visions.

This is what Isaiah heard when God said " make the people to hear and not comprehend and make them see and not perceive and so their hearts failed to understand. "

Isaiah 6: 9 - 10

And he said, Go, and tell this people, Hear ye indeed, but understand not; and see ye indeed, but perceive not. Make the heart of this people fat, and make their ears heavy, and shut their eyes; lest they see with their eyes, and hear with their ears, and understand with their heart, and convert, and be healed.

These are the curses termed generational curses because of our inability to receive and comprehend directions and God's counsel.

www.ingramcontent.com/pod-product-compliance
Lightning Source LLC
Chambersburg PA
CBHW052204150726
48002CB00003B/1119